TO PRC
AFRESH

TO PROCLAIM AFRESH

DECLARATION AND OATHS FOR CHURCH OF ENGLAND MINISTERS

The Faith and Order Commission
of the Church of England

CHURCH HOUSE PUBLISHING

Church House Publishing
Church House
Great Smith Street
London SW1P 3AZ

www.chpublishing.co.uk

Published 2022 for the Faith and Order Commission
of the Church of England by Church House Publishing

British Library Cataloguing in Publication Data

A catalogue record for this book is available
from the British Library

Typeset by ForDesign

Printed in the UK by XXXXo

Contents

Foreword by the Archbishop of Canterbury

The Declaration of Assent and Oaths are something I use a lot in my role. I find the words of the Declaration are ones that have a degree of poetry and resonance about them. I suspect many bishops like me will have used elements of the Declaration in many sermons as priests are being licensed in a wide variety of situations. It is therefore very good indeed that this booklet explores the history and theology of the Declaration and the Oaths. As well as being documents much used by some they will equally be little known by others and many of us will not know the history or have considered carefully the theology and other issues of a cultural nature, for example, around the use of oaths.

This short booklet sets out to dig deep into the significance of the Declaration and Oaths, to help all those taking the Declaration and Oaths to explore how they came about, how they connect us to the wider Church and to one another.

This study starts with history, because the Declaration and Oaths are steeped in our history as a Church and connect us to the Church throughout the ages. So if they feel strange, or even challenging to understand or absorb, it is because we do not stand alone in our time of history, but are part of something bigger than ourselves; they were formed in a time much different from ours, and the historical section helps understand the imagination that gave birth to them. The rest of the document then explores how we make sense of them for today, in ways that enrich our understanding of ministry and the relationship between minister and national Church, local church and wider Church.

The Declaration itself is a compact theological text that draws together some essential threads of what it means to be Anglican, and how we express this Anglican identity – through our liturgy, our Scriptures, our Creeds and our historical formularies. The Oaths, for themselves, may be something that many would-be ministers have pondered, and at times felt uneasy about. Neither allegiance nor obedience are popular terms in contemporary culture, particularly as we are, rightly, concerned about possible abuses of power. How do we understand what happens in the Oaths? How does our own cultural background differ from that of the time when these were conceived, and how do we understand and appropriate them faithfully, responsibly, and with integrity for today? The chapter on the Oaths is not merely theoretical, but also considers some of the practical questions often asked around swearing versus affirming, citizenship, or the limits of the Oaths.

The final chapter concludes with reflections on what happens when we make the Declaration and take these Oaths in concrete settings, in ordinations, in services of inauguration of ministry or in consecrations: what kind of relationships are created? What kind of expectations? How do they fit within the overall liturgy? This concluding chapter unpacks the concrete meaning and significance of making the Declaration and taking the Oaths, and the power of language and symbol, so that those who have not taken them before, or maybe have taken them without much consideration, can come to appreciate the power and weight of what the moment means.

While this booklet has ordinands and those preparing for lay ministry in mind, I very much hope it will help the whole Church to come to a deeper appreciation of this part of the tradition that we hold together.

The Most Revd and Rt Hon. Justin Welby

Archbishop of Canterbury

Preface

by the Chair of the Faith and Order Commission

The work of the Faith and Order Commission of the Church of England is often commissioned by the Archbishops, the House of Bishops, the General Synod or the Council for Christian Unity. Sometimes, however, the Commission itself decides that a particular area of the Church's life and witness should command its attention. This report on the Declaration and Oaths falls into the latter category. Members of the Commission felt that there is a depth of significance and richness of meaning in the Declaration and Oaths that is not always fully apprehended by those required to make them, especially those who do so for the first time.

The Commission now offers this analysis and commentary on The Declaration of Assent and Oaths to the Church in the hope that we may better understand their place in our calling to proclaim the gospel of our Lord Jesus Christ to 'this generation' in obedience to God who has given us a place in this 'part of the One, Holy, Catholic and Apostolic Church'.

The Right Reverend Dr Christopher Cocksworth

Chair of the Faith and Order Commission

Chapter 1   The Declaration of Assent

Historical background

The Church of England – like almost all churches – requires its ministers to assent to a formal body of Christian teaching. These commitments assist the health and unity of the Church, in the midst of its diversity, and help to guarantee that the Christian message is taught in every parish. Authorized ministers – whether clergy or laity – are not at liberty to believe and teach anything they choose. These corporate commitments are expressed in the 1975 Preface and Declaration of Assent:

> **Preface:** *The Church of England is part of the One, Holy, Catholic and Apostolic Church, worshipping the one true God, Father, Son and Holy Spirit. It professes the faith uniquely revealed in the Holy Scriptures and set forth in the catholic creeds, which faith the Church is called upon to proclaim afresh in each generation. Led by the Holy Spirit, it has borne witness to Christian truth in its historic formularies, the Thirty-nine Articles of Religion,* The Book of Common Prayer *and the Ordering of Bishops, Priests and Deacons. In the declaration you are about to make, will you affirm your loyalty to this inheritance of faith as your inspiration and guidance under God in bringing the grace and truth of Christ to this generation and making Him known to those in your care?*

> **Declaration:** *I, A B, do so affirm, and accordingly declare my belief in the faith which is revealed in the Holy Scriptures and set forth in the catholic creeds and to which the historic formularies of the Church of England bear witness; and in public prayer and administration of the sacraments, I will use only the forms of service which are authorized or allowed by Canon.*

The Declaration of Assent is made whenever clergy are ordained, instituted, installed, licensed or admitted to other public office in the Church (Canon C 15). Most clergy therefore will make this Declaration on many occasions during their ministries. Similarly, Readers and other licensed lay workers make the Declaration (omitting mention of the sacraments) when they are admitted and licensed. The Preface and Declaration of Assent, agreed by the Church of England's General Synod in 1975, were born out of the theological conversations of the 1960s.[1] Understanding the Declaration's origins is important for appreciating its distinctive emphases, including its purpose and shape.

The doctrinal commitments of the Church of England were recast and renewed in the light of developments in understanding Holy Scripture during the sixteenth-century Reformation, expressed in summary form in the Thirty-nine Articles of Religion. These were promulgated under Elizabeth I in 1571, reaffirmed at the Restoration in 1662, and for centuries have been published in a single volume with the Book of Common Prayer and the Ordinal. Taken together, these three historic texts (often called 'formularies') remain the formal and legal basis of Church of England teaching. The canons declare:

> *The Thirty-nine Articles are agreeable to the Word of God and may be assented unto with a good conscience by all members of the Church of England. (Canon A 2)*

> *The doctrine of the Church of England is grounded in the Holy Scriptures, and in such teachings of the ancient Fathers and Councils of the Church as are agreeable to the said Scriptures. In particular such doctrine is to be found in the Thirty-nine Articles,* The Book of Common Prayer, *and the Ordinal. (Canon A 5)*

From the 1570s, subscription to the Thirty-nine Articles was expected of all Church of England clergy (and some other groups like schoolteachers, and members of Oxford and Cambridge universities). The precise form of subscription varied over the years. By the canons of 1604, all clergy had to affirm 'willingly and *ex animo*' – that is, 'from the heart', without mental reservation – that the Articles were 'agreeable to the Word of God'.[2] This was altered in Victorian times by the 1865 Clerical Subscription Act to the following form:

> *I, A B, do solemnly make the following declaration: I assent to the Thirty-nine Articles of Religion, and to the Book of Common Prayer and of the ordering of bishops, priests, and deacons. I believe the doctrine of the Church of England as therein set forth, to be agreeable to the Word of God; and in public prayer and administration of the sacraments I will*

use the form in the said book prescribed and none other, except so far as shall be ordered by lawful authority.

One hundred years later, in the 1960s, this Declaration was still in force but increasingly under pressure from clergy who found it problematic or a burden to their conscience. Some protested publicly at being required to subscribe in this form, which brought the doctrinal discipline of the Church of England into disrepute.

Among twentieth-century Anglicans, across the globe, there was a very wide range of views concerning the Thirty-nine Articles. Some rejoiced in them as a beautiful and succinct summary of Anglican doctrine and the best expression of Anglican theological identity. Others were dissatisfied with them on the following grounds:

- The Articles assume an Augustinian/Reformed theological framework.
- The Articles offer propositional teaching, not fluid theology which wrestles with puzzles and perplexities.
- The Articles focus on Reformation questions concerning justification and the sacraments.
- The Articles are polemical, pointing out the errors of other Christians.
- The Articles belong to a very different cultural and philosophical context, with no consideration either of more recent questions such as the secular state, urbanization, technology, race, ecumenism, other religions, lay ministry, or of the gifts of the Holy Spirit.[3]

The place of the Articles in modern Anglicanism was a major debate at the Lambeth Conference in 1968. There was increasingly diverse practice around the Anglican Communion – some provinces retained the Articles in their constitutions, while others revised them, replaced them or abandoned them altogether. Some have never adopted them in the first place.

The Church of England's Doctrine Commission considered these questions in *Subscription and Assent to the Thirty-nine Articles* (1968). They concluded that revising the Articles, or replacing them with a new authoritative doctrinal statement which would gain the enthusiastic backing of the whole Church of England, would be too difficult, too lengthy, and itself soon out of date. Abandoning subscription to the Articles altogether would also be counterproductive, as it would give the impression that the Church of England was not concerned for the biblical faith of its ministers. Therefore, the Doctrine Commission proposed a new approach to subscription which, if it was to win wide acceptance, must satisfy several conditions:

- It must recognize that the Articles are a historic document and should be interpreted only within their historical context.
- It must leave room for an appeal to the Articles as a norm within Anglican theology.
- It must not tie down the person using it to acceptance of every one of the Articles of 1571.
- It must preserve the comprehensiveness characteristic of the Church of England.
- It must not put the Articles in isolation, but must acknowledge that Bible, Creeds, Prayer Book, Ordinal and the developing consensus of Anglican thought also have their own contribution to make to the doctrine of the Church of England. It must also indicate that these possess different degrees of authority.
- It must not only declare in what ways the Church of England is distinctive, but must indicate the doctrines it shares with all Christians.
- The possibility of fresh understandings of Christian truth must be explicitly left open.[4]

The agreed way forward was for the new Declaration of Assent to be kept very brief, but now introduced by a fuller Preface which sets out the context in which the Declaration is to be understood. This was intended to allow a more open interpretation of the historic Reformation formularies and to make clear that the Church of England is both *reformata* (reformed) and *semper reformanda* (always to be reformed; or 'always patient at being reformed'). Thus clergy and licensed lay ministers continue to affirm their loyalty to the classic doctrine of the Church of England, while also being guaranteed liberty to ask new doctrinal questions.[5]

Commentary

The Preface to the Declaration of Assent is read by a bishop, archdeacon, registrar or other authorized person before services of ordination, and every time a new ministry is inaugurated. It is carefully designed, and is noteworthy both for its brevity (only 134 words) and its comprehensiveness. It points beyond itself to other texts and formularies, though without prescribing particular interpretations of those texts. In that sense the Preface is deliberately wide, while nevertheless clearly marking the ground upon which the Church of England stands. Each phrase deserves study and reflection.

The Church of England is part of the One, Holy, Catholic and Apostolic Church ...

The Preface begins with a statement which is humble, modest and self-restrained, yet also confident and assured. Canon A 1, the first of the Church of England's canons, states that the Church of England 'belongs' to the 'true and apostolic Church of Christ.' The Preface expands this idea by enumerating the four classic 'marks' of the Church – one, holy, catholic, apostolic – as found in the Nicene Creed. So it locates us immediately in this universal Church, which stretches back to the age of the early Fathers and the Ecumenical Councils, not in any subdivision or modern grouping of Christians.

But the Preface is modest, because it tells us clearly that the Church of England is not equivalent with or equal to the whole Church, but is only a part or portion of it. It is a part of something greater than itself; it exists only because the greater thing, the universal Church, the one Church of Jesus Christ, exists. By the Church of England's very existence as a part of a greater whole, it points to something beyond itself. As Michael Ramsey wrote in his classic study of Anglicanism, the Church of England 'is not sent to commend itself as "the best type of Christianity," but by its very brokenness to point to the universal Church wherein all have died'.[6]

This modesty – this sense of the Church of England's incompleteness – is balanced in the Preface by confidence. By asserting plainly that the Church of England is part of the one, holy, catholic and apostolic Church, we are assured that (however imperfectly) within its life, the true Church of Jesus Christ is to be found. There is both a positive and a defensive aspect to the statement.

Positively, we are to trust that the Church of England's teaching, ministry and sacraments are those of the catholic Church. Defensively, we cannot agree with any suggestion that the Church of England is lacking anything required to be authentically a part of the Church of Jesus Christ. These claims by the Church of England do not stand in their own strength. Rather, they are true only insofar as the Church of England witnesses to the apostolic faith and shares in the apostolic ministry. In this sense, both the modesty ('part') and the confidence ('is') of the opening words of the Preface are interdependent.

... worshipping the one true God, Father, Son and Holy Spirit ...

From telling us what the Church of England is, the Preface next tells us what the Church of England does. Worship appears, significantly, very early in the text (and indeed, when read aloud, the emphasis naturally falls upon the word 'worshipping'). The obligation to worship God is laid upon God's people throughout the Bible. A primary way the Church of England has expressed and communicated the faith has been through its worship and liturgy, such as *The Book of Common Prayer*.

The Preface orientates us firmly towards God, to glorify God. The Church exists in order to offer worship, before it exists to do anything else. For Anglicans, the way we worship, our liturgy, is a source of life and teaching.

Who is worshipped? Not simply 'the one true God', but 'the one true God, Father, Son and Holy Spirit'. This explicit Trinitarian reference teaches us that Christians believe God is Trinity: there is no God who is not Father, Son and Spirit. As with the use of the Nicene formulary in the Preface's account of the Church, so this Trinitarian language anchors us in the patristic and conciliar age.

... It professes the faith uniquely revealed in the Holy Scriptures and set forth in the catholic creeds ...

After worship, the Preface turns to proclamation and teaching. The Church of England 'professes' the Christian faith. The term 'profess' has a wide range of meaning. In the Authorized Version, the people of Israel are called to 'profess' the history of their salvation as they enter the promised land (Deuteronomy 26.3), which other versions translate as 'declare'. It has the sense of speaking out and making known. We might think also of the *profession* of vows, such as marriage vows or those taken on entering the religious life. Here the word 'profess' has the sense of a firm public commitment or covenant. Again we are reminded that the Church of England's claims to be 'part' of the one Church of Jesus Christ can never simply be made as of right, but only insofar as it remains true to its profession. To profess the faith is to witness to Jesus Christ crucified and risen: this profession is the non-negotiable ground of the Church's life and being.

The faith which the Church of England professes is 'uniquely revealed' in the Holy Scriptures. *Sacra pagina*, the sacred page, is the privileged repository of the deposit of faith ('uniquely') and that faith is the fruit of divine initiative and divine gift ('revealed'). Of all the texts mentioned in the Preface, the Bible is given primary authority for the Church of England. What is revealed in the Scriptures is organized and distilled by the Early Church in the 'catholic' or ecumenical creeds (which are sometimes themselves called 'the profession of faith'). There is some debate about what is meant by 'the catholic creeds', which the Preface leaves undefined, but they are taken principally to mean the Nicene Creed and the Apostles' Creed.[7] Scripture and doctrine are thus held together. As Canon A 5 states: 'The doctrine of the Church of England is grounded in the Holy Scriptures, and in such teachings of the ancient Fathers and Councils of the Church as are agreeable to the said Scriptures.' The Preface makes the same claim.

... which faith the Church is called upon to proclaim afresh in each generation ...

The next phrase is vital in setting out the Church of England's mission, and is a key text in missional ecclesiology. As already seen, the Christian faith is given ('revealed'): it is the gospel of salvation, everlasting and unchanging. But 'to proclaim afresh in every generation' indicates that the twin tasks of evangelization and witness require attention to contemporary culture, and engagement with a constantly changing world. This section of the Preface provides the Church of England with the charter for its missional enterprise. It invites a constant dialogue and discernment about the relationship between the faith which is to be proclaimed and the fresh proclamation of that faith. It reminds us forcefully that the Church is called neither to nostalgia (as if the faith once proclaimed were now a fading memory) nor to novelty (as if the faith once proclaimed is insufficient for the present moment). Rather, following St Paul – who told the Corinthians, 'I received from the Lord what I also handed on to you' (1 Corinthians 11.23) – the Church of England is to hand on what has been received, with an apostolic zeal which is constantly renewed and refreshed by the power of the Holy Spirit. This is the true meaning of 'tradition' (from the Latin *traditio*, to hand down), as the Christian faith is passed from one generation to another.

In a world where we are increasingly aware of other cultures, and our own setting in England is increasingly multicultural, 'to proclaim afresh' needs to include engagement not just with our own surrounding culture, but also a willingness to learn from ways in which faith is proclaimed in the wider Church, and how the wider Church can help enrich, assist and, sometimes, correct our formulation of the faith for today.

Led by the Holy Spirit, it has borne witness to Christian truth ...

'Witness' is a key biblical concept in both Old and New Testaments. John the Baptist, for example, came as a 'witness' to testify to Jesus Christ (John 1.7). The apostles were commissioned as 'witnesses' to the suffering and resurrection of the Christ (Luke 24.48). Jesus Christ himself is called 'the faithful witness' (Revelation 1.5). Christian witness is about 'seeing and hearing and then saying'; it is a response to 'the goodness of God's transforming love'.[8] Those who witness always point away from themselves to God and the gospel of our Lord Jesus Christ.

In this task, the Church is 'led by the Holy Spirit'. Jesus Christ has promised to his followers that the Holy Spirit will make them witnesses 'to the ends of the earth' (Acts 1.8). The Holy Spirit, the chief witness to Christian truth, is the one who is the leader in witness. As Peter and the other apostles declared: 'we are witnesses to these things, and so is the Holy Spirit whom God has given to those who obey him' (Acts 5.32).

... in its historic formularies, the Thirty-nine Articles of Religion, The Book of Common Prayer *and the Ordering of Bishops, Priests and Deacons ...*

The three 'historic formularies' are part of the Church of England's witness, dating back to the sixteenth and seventeenth centuries. As witnesses, they do not point to themselves, or to the particularities of the Church of England's institutional life. They point away from themselves, towards the Christian faith of which they speak. The Thirty-nine Articles are doctrinal and propositional, *The Book of Common Prayer* and the Ordinal are liturgical, but all three are usually bound together in a single volume.

Doctrine and liturgy are interwoven. The Church of England expresses its doctrine in its liturgy, as truths about God lead naturally to praise and worship of God. For this reason, in the words of Canon B 5(3), liturgies 'shall be neither contrary to, nor indicative of departure from, the doctrine of the Church of England in any essential matter'. Ministers making the Declaration of Assent undertake to use 'only the forms of service which are authorized or allowed by canon'. The Church of England has approved a wide range of alternative liturgical material through its synodical and other instruments of governance, so there is a legitimate diversity in the conduct of public worship. Nevertheless, this commitment to using permitted liturgy is an important expression of the way in which, for the Church of England, worship, doctrine and church law are deeply interrelated.

The Ordinal marks the Church of England out as one that continues, and shares in, the threefold ministry of the pre-Reformation Church – bishops, priests and deacons. Each of the three orders is conferred by prayer and the laying-on of hands: deacons by the bishop; priests or presbyters by the bishop with fellow presbyters joining in the laying on of hands; bishops by other bishops (at least three). Each ordination rite is followed by the celebration of Holy Communion. So, again, by means of this ordered, liturgical and sacramental worship, preserving the essentials of primitive practice, the Church of England 'bears witness' to Christian truth.

... In the declaration you are about to make, will you affirm your loyalty to this inheritance of faith as your inspiration and guidance under God ...

In conclusion, the Preface asks a question of those to whom it is addressed. In keeping with the whole text, the question is a 'spacious' one. It asks for an affirmation of loyalty to 'this inheritance of faith', which consists in the Holy Scriptures, the catholic creeds and the historic Church of England formularies. Again it is important to note that candidates for ordination and licensing are not asked to assent to particular interpretations of these texts. It would be wrong, however, to read the question in a minimalist way, as if the Church of England asks little of its ministers by way of commitment to the faith they are entrusted to hand on. On the contrary, the Preface invites, on the part of those making the Declaration, deep familiarity with the various named witnesses – Scriptures, creeds and formularies – as their inspiration and guide.

... in bringing the grace and truth of Christ to this generation and making Him known to those in your care?

Finally, and importantly, the Preface ends with two interconnected exhortations to Church of England ministers – missional and pastoral. Christ is to be made known 'to those in your care'. Teaching, proclamation and the care (or, in older language, the 'cure') of souls go together. Although the Christian gospel is for the whole world, every Church of England minister is entrusted with a particular responsibility for a specific group of people (such as a parish or chaplaincy). Although the Christian gospel has been proclaimed for many centuries, our responsibility is for 'this generation'. The Preface ends with a strong Christological focus. Making Christ known is the minister's pastoral office. The pastor is ordained or licensed to proclaim Christ, the Good Shepherd, the one who is 'full of grace and truth' (John 1.14). All that the Preface gathers up – Holy Scriptures, catholic creeds, historic formularies – witness to Jesus Christ, and Church of England ministers are called to do likewise.

Discussion Questions

- 'One, holy, catholic and apostolic.' How do you understand these four 'marks of the Church' today?
- How does the Preface to the Declaration of Assent help us to understand the relationship between Scripture and Tradition?
- What is the value of the 'historic formularies' in the mission of the Church of England today?
- How does the Holy Spirit lead the Church's witness?
- What does it mean to 'proclaim afresh' in this generation?
- Why should we use only those forms of service which are 'authorized or allowed by canon'?

Chapter 2 The Oaths

All clergy and licensed lay ministers in the Church of England are required to swear two Oaths before they enter public office. The Oaths are taken before ordination and also before institution, installation, licensing or admission to any office in the Church – so most ministers will take these Oaths several times during their ministries.[9] The Oaths are distinct from the wide-ranging ordination promises which concern fundamental questions of Christian doctrine and Christian character. The specific context within which the Oaths are set – a loyalty to the inheritance of faith articulated in the Preface to the Declaration of Assent as discussed in Chapter 1 – should be remembered when interpreting their meanings.

Not every Christian Church has such oaths, but this is the way that, since the reformation era, the Church of England has ordered its life. The Oaths follow on from the profession of faith understood as a 'firm commitment or covenant' (discussed in Chapter 1). Loyalty to that inheritance of faith has a superiority to which allegiance and obedience should be aligned. The Oaths should therefore be understood in terms of the mission to which the profession of faith commits the Church.

The Oaths concern two specific relationships – an Oath of Allegiance to the sovereign and an Oath of Canonical Obedience to the bishop. These relational obligations would still remain, even if the act of oath-taking did not occur. All citizens of the United Kingdom (including the clergy) are expected to pay allegiance to the crown, even if they have not taken a public Oath of Allegiance. Similarly, all clergy of the Church of England are expected to pay canonical obedience to their bishop, even if by some oversight they avoided the public Oath of Obedience. Dispensing with the Oaths would not dispense with the obligations. However, in taking the Oaths, something important is happening. Ministers are making a public promise, articulating basic obligations and committing to certain relationships – with the sovereign, the bishop and, by implication, the whole Church.

A parallel is the Official Secrets Act, part of the law of the land. Members of the government, or the security and intelligence services, with access to national secrets are required to sign a statement promising not to betray that confidential information. But they are still bound to protect national secrets whether or not they have promised to do so in writing. 'Signing' the Official Secrets Act is a formal and symbolic reminder of these wider responsibilities. In the same way, taking the Oath of Allegiance and the Oath of Canonical Obedience reminds Church of England ministers – every time they enter a new sphere of ministry – of their obligations.

The Oaths make personal and specific what is already true about the relationship of Church of England ministers to the sovereign and to the Church, represented by a bishop. They are intended to deepen trust in relationships, not merely in the one making the promise, but also in the one receiving the promise and the wider Church they represent.

To consider in what way the Oaths can yield blessings, we need to think about what 'allegiance' and 'obedience' require and, also, what they do *not* require. These two terms will be considered generally first and then, specifically, in terms of the Oaths themselves.

Allegiance and obedience

In general terms, Christians have various kinds of *allegiance*. For example, they may have allegiance to their country, to a certain geographical area (a diocese, region, city, town or village), or perhaps some social cause concerned with compassion and justice. Allegiance, in this sense, is to do with committing to the people, places and causes which we love or care about. Practically speaking, allegiance becomes active when, for example, Christians are called on to make a decision about how best to serve their local environment in the face of some proposal for change (e.g. an affordable housing development). Allegiance itself is only the beginning. A process of critical thought is required about how to embody that allegiance by one course of action or another.

Similarly, Christians are called to a variety of relationships which involve *obedience.* To obey is to accord the direction of your reasoning and will with that of another – for example, a person, a community or a law. In itself, obedience is morally neutral. It is what obedience requires, along with its relational context and purpose, which give to obedience its moral significance. We see this when we consider the laws of God. Jesus said all the Law and the prophets depend upon two commandments: 'love the Lord your God with all your heart, and with all your soul, and with all your mind' and 'love your neighbour as yourself' (Matthew 22.37–40). Love is the obedient form of relationships between God, self and neighbour. The purpose of obedience, therefore, is a unified relationship of love between all three.

However, just what such obedient love means in practice needs some working out. Obedience for Christians must not be unreflective but instead should be deliberative and discerning, as our reasoning and will are deployed in God's service. How to obey the double love command does not simply drop out of thin air, but requires critical thought. Should a Church of England primary school, for which a cleric is a governor, become an academy or remain in its current status? Should a patch of land belonging to the church be sold for housing development – and if it is sold, on what basis? Submitting these questions to the double love commandment provides a framework for reasoning but not immediate answers.

Of course, not every relationship requires the same kind of obedience – and certainly not complete obedience. Obedience to the Word of God is distinct from other kinds of obedience, just as loyalty to the inheritance of faith takes primacy over other kinds of allegiance. While it will commonly be unproblematic to obey a wide range of laws and regulations, a call to obedience to anyone or anything other than the Word of God invites the question: 'Should we obey?' In the armed services, for example, personnel may rightly question whether the commands they have received are lawful. In a civilian context, whether one obeys an order to run would depend on who gives the order (e.g. a uniformed officer leading people away from a fire).

If we are to obey, the next question is: '*How* should we obey?' To which developer should the land be sold, for example? This is a matter of discerning deliberation that aims to answer the question: 'What now should I do?' In general terms, therefore, allegiance and obedience both involve Christians reflecting and deliberating about what is and is not required of them. They do not, except in certain emergency circumstances, involve being 'blind', as in the common phrases 'blind obedience' or 'blind allegiance'.

Avoiding 'blind' obedience, or unquestioning loyalty, is particularly important in preventing the development of a culture in which such obedience and loyalty are turned to sinful purposes. In cases of bullying, abuse or other misuses of power, it is common that the person suffering this abuse, and often bystanders too, initially have difficulty in recognizing what was going on in a given relationship. One of the factors that can make that recognition difficult is precisely the loyalty, trust and obedience that were important elements of the relationship. This does not mean that loyalty, trust and obedience are inherently problematic. But it does suggest that reflective, deliberative obedience, and willingness to question and challenge, depend in part upon the quality of a church's culture. To become sustained aspects of ecclesial life, these tasks have to be properly embedded, enabling honest explorations of the forms of power in the life of the church, and allow for widespread communication and education about those forms of power and the problems to which they are prone. There also need to be easily available forms of support and advice for those beginning to question relationships in which something seems to be going wrong and those in positions of authority should not be defensive when challenged and questioned but take such critique seriously.

In summary, the taking of the Oaths is an opportunity to focus our minds on how allegiance and obedience, which come as part and parcel of certain offices in the Church of England, order the Church's life. What is required of those taking the Oaths? What freedoms, within the ordered life of the Church, do the Oaths imply? How can sin distort and corrupt relationships of obedience and allegiance? Next we consider each of the Oaths in turn by examining how they should be read in the context of the specific relationships they address.

The Oath of Allegiance

The Oath of Allegiance was introduced in the 1580s at a period of national crisis, when there was a succession of political plots to overthrow Queen Elizabeth I. Some clergy in the Church of England were involved in these schemes, hoping to dismantle the Elizabethan Reformation and return the nation to Roman Catholicism, perhaps under Mary Queen of Scots as a new monarch. Therefore an Oath of Allegiance was introduced to prevent clergy from undermining the crown and thereby also undermining the Church.[10] An identical Oath is taken by other office holders in public life, including Members of Parliament, mayors, members of the judiciary and army officers, and by those taking on British citizenship in a citizenship ceremony.

The Oath reads as follows (see Canon C 13):

> I, A B, *do swear that I will be faithful and bear true allegiance to Her*
> *Majesty Queen Elizabeth II, her heirs and successors, according to law:*
> *So help me God.*

We are not now in a similar position to the late sixteenth century and so the particular concerns which motivated oath-taking then do not apply exactly now. How then should we understand it today? The Oath of Allegiance is made in the context of modern UK society and government, a democracy in which government is conducted by ministers through Parliament. The Oath is made to one who is a ruler, but whose rule is exercised through Parliament, which is in effect supreme. By long-standing convention, the sovereign follows the advice of the prime minister. This means that the Oath is an affirmation of one's place in this society and its laws.

Some have queried the rightness of an Oath to the sovereign. Nonetheless, the Oath has an honoured place in the life of the Church of England and at its best aims at what might be called 'the blessings of allegiance'. The relationship between Church and state is configured differently in different parts of the Anglican Communion, with each local context shaped by different histories and cultures. In England, the shape of relationship that we have inherited is establishment, as a gift and an opportunity. The taking of the Oath should be seen within the constitutional context of the UK, whereby the monarch does not and may not express a personal opinion on any matter directly related to their exercise of that office. In context, the Oath of Allegiance can reasonably be understood to function as a reminder to the Church – both those swearing the Oath and those witnessing it – of certain blessings of the relationship to which it refers. These blessings come in at least two forms: mutual loyalty and missional unity.

The blessings of allegiance: mutual loyalty

First, there is a blessing of mutual loyalty. When someone swears faithful and true allegiance to the sovereign, they should do so not as a formality to be quickly finished but as a commitment to an enduring relationship. That relationship involves a mutual loyalty of one party to the other as each commits to play their part in the relationship. The result is that trust may grow between them and blessings may follow for others.

The allegiance to which the oath-taker commits is informed by the promises made at the sovereign's own crowning. In the Coronation Oath, specified in the 1688 Succession Act, the sovereign is asked the following questions, among others, by the Archbishop and answers affirmatively, thereby making a solemn promise:

> *Will you to the utmost of your power maintain the Laws of God and the true profession of the Gospel?*
>
> *Will you to the utmost of your power maintain in the United Kingdom the Protestant Reformed Religion established by law?*
>
> *Will you maintain and preserve inviolably the settlement of the Church of England, and the doctrine, worship, discipline, and government thereof, as by law established in England?*
>
> *And will you preserve unto the Bishops and Clergy of England, and to the Churches there committed to their charge, all such rights and privileges, as by law do or shall appertain to them or any of them?*[11]

The Oath of Allegiance to the sovereign by Church of England ministers should be understood within this broader context. On this view, every time an ordinand, member of the clergy or licensed lay minister makes the Oath of Allegiance to the sovereign, there is an interlocking of these promises, forming and reaffirming the mutual loyalty which lies between the sovereign and the Church of England. In this way, the relationship between the parties is sealed and renewed regularly with this Oath.[12] Again, as with the profession of faith, it makes sense to think of this mutual loyalty in terms of a firm commitment or covenant. Understood like this, the Oath is a way in which loyalty to the inheritance of faith has taken form in institutional practice. Moreover, the Oath of Allegiance specifies that the Oath is with the sovereign's 'heirs and successors, according to law' – that is, according to the lawful line of succession. And so the covenantal relationship is one which forms a loyal bridge of trust between sovereigns, which is not even broken by death. The allegiance is not simply to the person of the sovereign but, more fundamentally, to the office they hold.

For those who find such a way of understanding this Oath compelling – and there will, quite reasonably, be some who do not – it may also be useful to think of the Oath in the performative terms which will be developed in chapter 3. On this view, the Coronation Oath may be understood as an underlying, worshipful keynote sustained over decades, to which the many Oaths of Allegiance made on various occasions join in to make one harmonious and concordant melody, resounding with the gospel of Christ. The Coronation Oath might be read out or printed in churches from time to time (for example, ahead of a new minister's arrival) to remind the congregation of the context in which the Oath of Allegiance is made.

The Blessings of Allegiance: Missional Unity

Second, there is the blessing of missional unity. The Coronation Oath requires a solemn Christian commitment to maintain 'the Laws of God the true Profession of the Gospel and the Protestant Reformed Religion Established by Law'. This commitment covers the whole of the land of England, united as a single field of mission under the crown.[13] In pledging allegiance to the sovereign, ordinands and other ministers swearing the Oath celebrate that royal commitment to God's mission to bring good news to England. On this view, making the Oath of Allegiance is, therefore, an entirely apt commitment for those pledging their loyalty to the inheritance of faith spoken of in the Preface and Declaration of Assent. Moreover, whenever the Oath is made by those who are ordained, in parish after parish at a new institution, installation, licensing or admission to some church office, there is an implied renewal of this national mission among 'the Churches committed to their Charge', as the Coronation Oath puts it. The Oath, understood in this way, has the potential to strengthen a sense of common mission and purpose, binding together all the members of the Church of England. Such allegiance, when articulated and heard by ordained and lay together, does not, as noted above, answer immediately the question of what is to be done in mission. Instead, it may inspire oath-takers and those who witness the Oath to answer it for themselves. A public taking or performance of the Oath, a theme to be addressed in Chapter 3, is therefore important for its missional significance.

Taken in this way, the Oath of Allegiance has not been primarily bound up with an individual sovereign at any one point in history – their personal beliefs or way of life – but rather it has been about the intertwining of one's life with the corporate body of the Church, whose head is Jesus Christ. In Christ the whole body is built up as each part does its work (Ephesians 4.15–16). This Oath can help the Church to realize this truth. Sovereigns, bishops, clergy and licensed lay ministers take oaths that point beyond themselves, directing the vision of the people of God beyond each of these offices to the inheritance of faith and to the highest authority from whom the call and mission of the Church of England proceeds, the God and Father of our Lord Jesus Christ.

In summary, if the loyalty called for in the Preface and Declaration of Assent is to the Church's inheritance of faith, then the loyalty called for in the Oath of Allegiance is to the sovereign who also promises at their coronation to maintain that faith.

Questions and concerns about the Oath of Allegiance

The requirement for all Church of England ministers to swear the Oath of Allegiance is, however, not without its difficulties. A number of reasonable questions have been raised about the Oath's role and significance in the life of the Church of England:

(i)   Should the Church of England and the state be intertwined?

(ii)   Can republicans minister in the Church of England?

(iii)   What about ministers who have moved to England from other nations?

(i)   Should the Church of England and the state be intertwined?

Others might be concerned about swearing allegiance to a sovereign in the context of the Church's life. It may be that they find the Oath surprising and incongruous since it is not clear what the monarch, who is perhaps more commonly thought of in terms of a state and societal role, has to do with the day-to-day life of the Church of England. In fact, as well as being the head of state, the sovereign holds the titles 'Defender of the Faith and Supreme Governor of the Church of England'. The sovereign carries out a number of duties that are important to the life of the Church of England – for example, the appointment, after the due processes of the Church's nomination have been completed, of Archbishops and Bishops and the inauguration of General Synod.

A concern about the intertwining of state and Church could, however, take a more political form. Pacifist members of the Church may be concerned about the role of the sovereign as head of the armed forces. Others might be concerned that the Church's supreme governor has given royal assent to Acts of Parliament which do not accord with the Coronation Oath to 'maintain the laws of God and the true profession of the Gospel' or to 'cause Law and Justice, in Mercy, to be executed in all your judgements'. In other words, the entanglement of the monarchy with the procedures of the government might make one due to swear the Oath doubtful. However, with respect to legislation at least, this would be to misunderstand the relationship between the monarch and Parliament. More narrowly, it is simply not known to what extent the monarch laments or celebrates any particular Act to which they give assent.[14] More broadly, the sovereign's standing as supreme governor of the Church of England, with its calling to profess the unchanging gospel, in no way implies the Church's endorsement of the policies of particular governments which, while raised up by God (Romans 13.1), yet come and go with the passing of time.

(ii)   Can republicans minister in the Church of England?

Some ministers may have doubts about the very institution of monarchy itself, and therefore about swearing the Oath of Allegiance. However, it should be remembered that the Oath is to the sovereign, not to the principle of monarchy or any other theory of government. It is a matter of fact that the sovereign has a role in the governance of the United Kingdom, and is supreme governor of the Church of England. This is the constitution and the national context within which the Church of England bears witness. That is not to say that ministers are forbidden from proposing different ways in which the state or Church should be governed, for example as a republic or with the Church of England disestablished. Allegiance to the sovereign should not be blind or uncritical. Instead, there should always be an openness to what God is saying to the Church and nation today.

(iii)   What about ministers who have moved to England from other nations?

The Oath of Allegiance is only required for Church of England ministers who are citizens of the United Kingdom, or of nations in the British Commonwealth where the Queen is head of state. For those who are citizens of other nations, a legal exception is provided, at the bishop's discretion.[15]

The Oath of Canonical Obedience

The Oath of Obedience to the bishop is an ancient, pre-Reformation oath (though the earliest known example in print, in the original Latin, is from 1713).[16] The Church of England canons describe the Oath as belonging to 'the ancient law and usage of this Church and Realm of England' (Canon C 1, paragraph 3). Its origins are lost in the mists of time, but probably stretch back to feudal society when local inhabitants owed obedience to the lord of the manor, or to the Lord Bishop. One historian of canon law observes:

> The oath of canonical obedience is ... essentially an oath of vassalage which along with some other things, has somehow managed to survive the demise of medieval feudalism more or less unscathed. Much of the confusion which surrounds it today must be attributed to the demise of the context in which it was devised, with the result that no-one is quite sure what effect it is supposed to have in the modern world.[17]

The Oath reads as follows (see Canon C 14):

> *I, A B, do swear by Almighty God that I will pay true and canonical obedience to the Lord Bishop of X and his successors in all things lawful and honest: So help me God.*

The Oath is made to an individual person, who is responsible (like a magistrate in secular affairs) for administering the laws of the Church. Yet the Oath is not attached to that person but to their office – it is not to 'Bishop N' but to 'The Lord Bishop of X'. Clergy do not retake the Oath when a new bishop comes to the diocese. Nor does the Oath depend upon the personal virtues or opinions of the current occupant of the see. Rather it is a symbolic way of expressing loyalty to the historic and corporate teaching of the Church of England – loyalty to the inheritance of faith. Bishops themselves swear canonical obedience, to the Archbishop of Canterbury or York.

How should this Oath be interpreted in our twenty-first-century context? There are two important aspects, considered in terms of blessings and limits.

The blessings of godly authority

As noted above, obedience to authority is often an unpopular teaching. Indeed, those in authority need to be challenged and removed if they become abusive, corrupt or simply incompetent. The account of obedience given at the start of this chapter implies just this possibility: namely that a minister's obedience should not be 'blind' but rather informed and, where appropriate, critical. A minister has liberty to ask questions such as, 'Should I obey?' and, 'If I should obey, how?'

Nonetheless obedience to authority is a frequent biblical injunction – for example, Christian children are instructed to obey their parents (Ephesians 6.1). When those in authority are godly and wise, obedience brings much blessing. The apostles teach Christians to respect and obey leaders within the local church: 'We appeal to you, brothers and sisters, to respect those who labour among you, and have charge of you in the Lord and admonish you; esteem them very highly in love because of their work' (1 Thessalonians 5.12–13); and the Letter to the Hebrews puts it this way: 'Obey your leaders and submit to them, for they are keeping watch over your souls and will give an account. Let them do this with joy and not with sighing – for that would be harmful to you' (Hebrews 13.17). These texts assume that respect for Christian leaders is a vital aspect of healthy church life, and that Christian community life should aim to avoid causing unnecessary 'sighing' among leaders (who work hard caring for the community) and instead give them reasons for 'joy'. The rationale is that leaders who are weighed down will be less able to bring the blessings the church needs. Here is a beautiful picture of healthy dynamics in the local congregation. In an episcopally ordered Church we can extrapolate this biblical principle, not only of local congregations in obedience to their clergy, but also of clergy in obedience to their bishops.

The Church of England ordination service distils this relational principle. In *The Book of Common Prayer* ordinal, presbyters are asked:

> Will you reverently obey your Ordinary, and other chief ministers, unto whom is committed the charge and government over you; following with a glad mind and will their godly admonitions, and submitting yourselves to their godly judgments?

Again, the picture is of healthy relationships. When the bishop offers 'godly' counsel and instruction, the clergy rejoice and promise to obey – not grudgingly, or with grumbling, but 'with a glad mind and will'. This is not just about the harmonious internal administration of the Church of England, but is a spiritual discipline. The *Common Worship* ordinal includes similar questions:

> To deacons: 'Will you accept the discipline of this Church and give due respect to those in authority?'

> To presbyters: 'Will you accept and minister the discipline of this Church, and respect authority duly exercised within it?'

> To bishops: 'Will you accept the discipline of this Church, exercising authority with justice, courtesy and love, and always holding before you the example of Christ?'

Bishops are also required to submit to the discipline of the wider Church. The vocation of bishops is to model their ministry on that of Jesus Christ, 'the great shepherd of the sheep' (Hebrews 13.20), and will exercise authority in a just and loving manner. All Christians are inclined to sin, including bishops. That, in itself, does not qualify the status of the promises made.

The limits of clerical obedience

The Church of England, like every Church, has developed its own set of practical, household rules (out of the older body of Western canon law) – 'the canons', the rules in the form of law, which are bound up with the law of the land – are designed to order its life and help the Church flourish. These are not the only rules which do this, nor even the most important; they are those, however, by which the life of its ministers (ordained and lay) are governed. Obedience to the canons is made in the context of obedience to the bishop or their representative: it is thus an obedience which is both personal and institutional. The person to whom obedience is due is also under the same rules, and this limits the extent of obedience which may be called for. Without some practical rules there would be chaos and confusion. The canons help to provide structure and order, to avoid dissensions in the Church, and to foster mission. They are not intended as unnecessarily restrictive but as a set of parameters to help build healthy congregations and relationships of mutual, covenantal loyalty and trust.

The Oath of Obedience is carefully phrased. Clergy promise 'canonical obedience' – that is, obedience about matters covered by the canons – not blind, unthinking or wholesale obedience. The Oath is limited to 'all things lawful' – again a reference to canon law specifically, not obedience in all lawful things. This principle was laid down clearly by the Judicial Committee of the Privy Council in its 1863 judgment *Long vs Bishop of Cape Town*: 'the oath of canonical obedience does not mean that every clergyman will obey all the commands of the bishop against which there is no law, but that he will obey all such commands as the bishop by law is authorized to impose.'[18]

Many aspects of church life and mission are not governed by canon law, and here clergy have liberty to act as they and their congregations think best, even against the friendly advice of the bishop. But when a subject is covered explicitly by canon law, then the bishop's formal instructions are to be obeyed, although in some circumstances there may be a variety of ways of obeying among which clergy are free to choose. This carefully balanced combination of liberty and law, when it functions well, is the best of both worlds and a blessing to the Church.

One may look to a different time and context for an example. St Benedict gives an account of the monastic life in his Rule, in which obedience plays a foundational role. However, if brothers/sisters are faced with something beyond either their physical or moral capacity, they are to raise the matter with the abbot at an appropriate time 'without pride, obstinacy and refusal'.[19] Here is an example of obedience which gives place to an allowance of difficulties and respects the needs of those taking part in the promise. Moreover, obedience for St Benedict entails that both abbot and brothers/sisters obey in the context of listening to God in each other. In short, obedience may be seen in the context of the wider and deeper calling of the Church and individuals in Christ.

The Oath of Canonical Obedience takes for granted that those in authority are themselves obedient to the Christian message as proclaimed in the Word of God. The apostles expected loyalty, not to church leaders or canons, but first and foremost to the gospel of Jesus Christ. There is no place for obeying what is manifestly not according to the teaching of Christ. Canonical obedience therefore presupposes trust in the Church, its ways and its rites, that they guide people to follow Jesus Christ as Lord and Saviour. Obedience to bishops is an important aspect of right relationships in the Church, but comes a long way behind obedience to God.

The phrase 'lawful and honest' – or in the original Latin, *licitis et honestis* – has been widely debated. *Honestis* means something like respectable, honourable, worthy, virtuous, upright. This phrase reminds us that for Christians there is always something more important than being legally correct. Sometimes, even in the Church, laws are not virtuous and conflict with fundamental Christian principles, as has sadly occurred at various periods of Christian history. For the canons to be 'respectable', and deserving of honour, they will always promote Christian godliness and Christlike virtue. The Church of England's Oath of Canonical Obedience recognizes this deeper principle. Ultimately the clergy, like all Christians, answer to a higher tribunal. Ministers who have taken the Oath therefore have a responsibility to think carefully and prayerfully about what is lawful and honest in instructions they may receive.

All these caveats are important to bear in mind following the Independent Inquiry into Child Sexual Abuse (IICSA) and its pinpointing of a culture of deference as an obstacle to good safeguarding practices. To say that we need to address the problems of deference is not to argue against canonical obedience. Rather, it is to emphasize that unquestioning deference is not demanded by the Oaths. The spirit of the Oaths demands that clergy behave with integrity at all times, and this involves challenging oppressive, abusive or collusive practices that are the opposite of 'lawful and honest'.

Oath-taking and Christian discipleship

In conclusion, it is important to note that some ordinands and ministers will have concerns about whether oath-taking – to sovereign, bishop or both – is compatible with Christian discipleship. They recall that the New Testament warns explicitly against the swearing of oaths. In the Sermon on the Mount, Jesus Christ commands: 'Do not swear at all ... Let your word be "Yes, Yes" or "No, No", anything more than this comes from the evil one.' (Matthew 5.33–37). The apostle James reiterates the same teaching and warns that condemnation will fall on those who swear oaths (James 5–12).

However, within Anglican theology, these Bible passages have usually been understood to be a prohibition against rash or blasphemous swearing, not against the swearing of oaths in all circumstances. For example, the Thirty-nine Articles declare:

> As we confess that vain and rash Swearing is forbidden Christian men by our Lord Jesus Christ, and *James* his Apostle, so we judge that Christian religion doth not prohibit, but that a man may swear when the Magistrate requireth, in a cause of faith and charity, so it be done according to the Prophet's teaching in justice, judgement, and truth. (Article 39)

This is a reference to the Prophet Jeremiah, who taught that the Lord would be glorified among the nations if the people of Israel returned to the Lord, put away their ungodly practices, and only swore oaths 'in truth, in justice, and in uprightness' (Jeremiah 4.2). Here is biblical precedent for the swearing of oaths, provided those oaths are true, godly and to God's glory. Moreover, as the article implies, it can be argued that Jesus and James were criticizing the practice of swearing trivial and thoughtless oaths, rather than the swearing of oaths in solemn circumstances. Jesus himself may have taken an oath at his own trial (Matthew 26.63).[20]

Nonetheless, the interpretation of these various Bible passages has been a contested debate among Christians for many centuries. For that reason, the Oaths Act 1978 permits anyone in public life who objects to swearing an oath to instead make a 'solemn affirmation', which has the same legal force and effect as an oath. Clergy who, as a matter of theological conscience, would prefer not to 'swear by Almighty God' nor to follow their oath with 'So help me God', may substitute the following form of words:

> *I, A B, do solemnly, sincerely and truly declare and affirm that I will be faithful and bear true allegiance to Her Majesty Queen Elizabeth II, her heirs and successors, according to law.*

> *I, A B, do solemnly, sincerely and truly declare and affirm that I will pay true and canonical obedience to the Lord Bishop of X and his successors in all things lawful and honest.*

Discussion Questions

- What should 'obedience' and 'allegiance' mean in practice for a Christian?
- In what way, if at all, does taking the Oath of Allegiance to the sovereign make a difference to mission?
- Why are both canonical obedience and its limits important for a flourishing Church?
- How does 'loyalty to the inheritance of faith' relate to these Oaths?
- How might an understanding of the Oaths play a greater part in the life of your local church?

Chapter 3 The Declaration of Assent as enacted performance

The Declaration of Assent – which speaks of 'making Christ known' – is often made in the context of public worship. The preface to *Common Worship* (2000) notes that worship not only strengthens Christians for witness and service, but is itself a forum in which Christ is known. Furthermore, 'worship is more than what is said; it is also what is done and how it is done.'[21]

The Declaration of Assent is included as an adjunct to the *Common Worship* preface. This decision signals a number of things. First, although the Declaration is crucial for the life and work of the liturgical minister in the Church of England, it is not itself a piece of liturgy. Equally, the Declaration represents a kind of beginning – an appropriate introduction to, and summary of, what is later rehearsed in *Common Worship*'s liturgical word and gesture. Its prefatory position also indicates that the Declaration operates outside the structure, constraints and possibilities of liturgy but that it is the declarative condition of the minister's authorized liturgical life.

Given that the Declaration of Assent is both located at the outset of *Common Worship* and rehearsed at the outset of ordained ministry and at each subsequent appointment, it is clearly significant for the worshipping life of the minister and the ministry of the Church. What may be less clear to those invited to make the Declaration is its 'performative' and 'gestural' significance.

In pragmatic terms, an individual (or the representatives of a benefice to which they are to be licensed) might wish to treat the Declaration simply as something one must say in order to be licensed (or, indeed, ordained) in the Church of England. That is, the Declaration is sometimes wrongly treated as a kind of curiosity, of no great interest beyond being 'what one does' and (for those who take on new ministries) has to be done *repeatedly*. Rather than adding to its value, repetition is assumed to diminish the Declaration's significance. It is sometimes treated with a kind of sigh or shrug – a needful and necessary ritual, but a hoop one must jump through before getting on with the proper work of ministry.

This would be a misunderstanding of the power and dignity of the Declaration of Assent and its place in the life of the whole worshipping community. Just as worship is more than a formula of words, but is also a work of action or liturgical gesture, the Declaration is also a form of words which performs an action and is itself enacted. Its repetition at the outset of many ministries establishes it as a kind of foundational action for authorized service in the Church of England.

Word and action

The work of twentieth-century linguists and linguistic philosophers helpfully indicated the extent to which words may be actions and have a powerful 'performative' dimension. Here, 'performative' is taken to mean those kinds of statements and utterances that can bring about new states of affairs. In the first instance, these are utterances which in the very act of utterance 'do', 'perform' or 'enact' something. These utterances are contrasted with those that 'describe' or 'report' something, or are 'true or false'; performative utterances entail the doing of an action which would not *normally* be described as, or as 'just', saying something.

In the Preface to the Declaration of Assent, the minister is invited to 'affirm' and 'declare' their loyalty to the inheritance of faith as inspiration and guidance for their work of ministry in the communities they are about to serve. What kind of speech-act is the responding minister being invited to make? They reply, 'I … do so affirm, and declare …' and 'I will use …'. Certainly this 'declaration' is a statement. Arguably, however, it is no simple statement of fact. That is, those who make the Declaration, under the appropriate conditions, also act. When the minister makes the Declaration they enact something: their living commitment to the historic faith in Jesus Christ as it has been revealed in the life of the Church of England.

To say that making the Declaration of Assent is an action may seem like a trifling point. However, at the very least, it enables us to appreciate the profound seriousness of what is being said. The saying is a doing. This is something to which all those who make declarations (and, indeed, oaths) should be alert. It is a reminder that the notion of 'assent' is not simply a kind of 'nodding through'. When ministers are required to make the Declaration repeatedly it is not a mere formality or linguistic formula. It should more properly be read as a work in words, which both signals the profound commitment each minister offers to the life of work and witness in Jesus Christ, but also enacts commitment to the faith in Christ as it has been revealed within the life of the Church of England.

Liturgical and performative setting

The Declaration of Assent is a key moment in the life and work of Church of England ministers. The Oaths of Allegiance and Obedience are sworn publicly before a range of others present, prior to the service for ordinations, and as part of the service itself at the inauguration of a new ministry. Thus, for example, those to be consecrated bishop or suffragan bishop must make the Declaration 'publicly and openly' in the presence of 'the congregation there assembled'. The same applies when a bishop is enthroned in their cathedral, or when a suffragan bishop begins their ministry in a diocese, or on the first Sunday when a new minister begins with a congregation (if their licensing has taken place elsewhere). So, for example, ordinands often make the Declaration during their ordination service, but then repeat it during their first Sunday service in their curacy – again this is to be 'publicly and openly' in the presence of 'the congregation there assembled', not privately in the vestry (Canon C 15). The Declaration is not reserved simply for those who are ordained, but is also made by Readers as licensed ministers of the Word.

A number of things are clear from the public contexts in which the Declaration is rehearsed. The Declaration (like the Oaths) signifies changed public relationships and acquired responsibilities. It is no mere formula; it is an action that restates, rehearses and re-inscribes the relational character of ministry. The mutual accountability between bishop, minister and congregation is restated and reperformed in word in the presence of others. The minister's utterance signals their public commitment to the faith in Christ as it has been revealed within the life of the Church of England, held in common with the bishop and other ministers of God.

The presence of the congregation among whom a minister is to serve is hugely significant. The witness of the congregation is a signal not only of the public nature of licensed ministry, but that ministry is always located in community and comes with communal accountability. The minister is accountable to the community in which they are set; the minister's work is a public dimension of the life of the community they serve and lead. At the moment of Declaration the local congregation is the Church of England in that place, gathered and united in ministry and faith. The accountability expressed by the minister, in the company of bishop and congregation, is not simply to the local, but to the local as an expression of the one, holy, catholic and apostolic Church in that parish or place. The public Declaration of Assent acts as a token of doctrinal and liturgical trust; a public fostering of the shared belief and practice between minister and congregation.

That the Declaration of Assent is often located in the context of services of worship indicates that the fullest context of the minister's life is always one of worship and praise. Their work is located appropriately in the 'liturgy' (in Greek *leitourgia*), which means literally 'the people's work'. Even if they are set apart for a particular ministry, with specific responsibilities and accountability, they still remain members of the community which worships the Living God.

So why is the repeated public performance of the Declaration necessary? Why not make it a 'one-time deal'? Part of the answer to that question should already be clear: repetition is necessary when a minister takes up, for example, a new parish responsibility because the bishop, minister and congregation have entered into a new relationship with one another. The Declaration signifies publicly the new relationship, grounded in the mutual commitment to the deposit of faith and practice the Church of England has received.

There is, perhaps, a further horizon: if the repetition of the Declaration is always subtly different (a new parish ministry, for example, is never quite the same as the previous appointment), the restatement of the Declaration leaves its own incremental and beneficial deposit in the life and work of the minister and the Church. The life of a follower of Jesus is always a work of conversion to God. In the repetition and restatement of the Declaration, the community of believers is strengthened in the life they hold in common as they grow ever more into the likeness of Christ.

Conclusion

To repeat: words can be actions. The repeated restatement and re-enactment of the Declaration of Assent acts on and changes people, ministry and the Body of Christ. The responsibilities and relationships to which minister and congregation are called by the bishop are public, but they have personal implications. The words are always spoken and witnessed in particular places, at particular times, by particular people. They are living words which signal changed human realities.

That the proper occasion for the enactment and subsequent 're-enactment' or rehearsal of the Declaration of Assent is a liturgical one is entirely in keeping with the theological character of the Church of England. While the Declaration of Assent is positioned in the opening pages of *Common Worship*, its enactment and repetition within the context of worship reminds us that the Church of England finds its doctrinal dignity in its liturgical gesture and performance. The arrow of ministry through which Church of England ministers serve may be found in the principle *lex orandi, lex credendi* ('the law of praying is the law of believing'). The words of the Declaration of Assent and its repeated public performance are the still moment of focus, the taut bow and the action through which that arrow of love is released.

Discussion questions

- What surprises or challenges you, if anything, about understanding the Declaration and Oaths as enacted performance? Why?

- 'The repeated restatement and re-enactment of the Declaration of Assent acts on and changes people, ministry and the Body of Christ.' What, then, might be the personal implications for you and others in public ministry?

- '... ministry is always located in community and comes with communal accountability.' How do you understand 'communal accountability' in the light of what you have learned about the Oaths and Declarations from this chapter and others in this booklet?

Notes

1   For details of the synodical debates, see C. Podmore, 'The Church of England's Declaration of Assent', in *Aspects of Anglican Identity* (London: Church House Publishing, 2005), pp. 43–57.

2   Canon 36 of 1604, in G. Bray (ed.), *The Anglican Canons 1529–1947* (Woodbridge: Boydell Press, 1998), p. 321.

3   *Subscription and Assent to the Thirty-nine Articles: A Report of the Archbishops' Commission on Christian Doctrine* (London: SPCK, 1968), §63–9.

4   *Subscription and Assent*, §89.

5   *Subscription and Assent*, §94.

6   A. M. Ramsey, *The Gospel and the Catholic Church* (London: Longmans, Green, 1936; second edition, London: SPCK, 1990), p. 220.

7   For the place of the Athanasian Creed within modern Anglican identities, see J. Bennett, 'The Age of Athanasius: The Church of England and the Athanasian Creed, 1870–1873', *Church History and Religious Culture* (2017), pp. 220–47, and M. Davie, *The Athanasian Creed* (London: Latimer Trust, 2019).

8   Faith and Order Commission, *Witness* (London: Church House Publishing, 2020), p. 8.

9   Until the 1970s there was also a third Oath, against simony, by which clergy promised that they had not paid money, or offered other financial inducements, to secure preferment in the Church. The sin of simony (named after Simon Magus, who offered the apostles money in return for the gifts of the Holy Spirit, Acts 8.9–24) is of course still forbidden but is no longer endemic in the Church of England, so that Oath is no longer required.

10 For discussion of the history of the Oath, see R. Bursell, 'The Clerical Oath of Allegiance', *Ecclesiastical Law Journal* 17.3 (2015), pp. 295–305.

11 The form of the Oath reproduced here is the one used for the 1953 coronation. For the original, see Succession Act 1688.

12 Bray notes that 'It is perhaps not entirely irrelevant here to remember that in medieval theology, matrimony and ordination were mutually exclusive alternatives – a man could have one but not both. The justification for this was that ordination was marriage to the Church, and so the solemn vows taken at the time can legitimately be compared with those taken at a wedding ceremony' (G. Bray, *The Oath of Canonical Obedience* (London: Latimer Trust, 2004), fn10).

13 The Coronation Oath has varied over the centuries, and at different times has also referred to Scotland, Ireland, Great Britain and the United Kingdom (G. Watt, 'The Coronation Oath', Ecclesiastical Law Journal 19.3 (2017); pp. 325–41, pp. 326–33). However, for present purposes, the focus here is the Church of England.

14 For discussion, see Watt, Coronation, pp. 325–41; pp. 340–1.

15 See section 2 of the Overseas and Other Clergy (Ministry and Ordination) Measure 1967: https://www.legislation.gov.uk/ukcm/1967/3/section/2, repeated in Canon C 13, paragraph 2.

16 E. Gibson, *Codex Juris Ecclesiastici Anglicani; or, The Statutes, Constitutions, Canons, Rubricks and Articles of the Church of England*, vol. 2 (London, 1713), p. 854.

17 Bray, *Canonical Obedience*, p. 12.

18 *The Reverend William Long v The Rt. Reverend Robert Gray D.D. Bishop of Cape Town (Cape of Good Hope)* [1864] UKPC 9 (24 June 1864) (bailii.org).

19 *The Rule of St. Benedict* (trans. Timothy Fry OSB, Collegeville, The Liturgical Press, 1981), MN chapter 68.

20 For further discussion, see Bray, *Canonical Obedience*, pp. 12–16.

21 *Common Worship: Services and Prayers for the Church of England* (London: Church House Publishing, 2000), p. ix.